GW00728151

THE
Apocraphya

THE
Apocraphya

GILLY SERGIEV

A GODSFIELD BOOK

Dedicated to all those who walk and talk the ways of peace.

First published in the U.K. in 2003
by Godsfield Press Ltd.,
Laurel House, Station Approach,
Alresford, Hampshire SO24 9JH, U.K.
www.godsfieldpress.com

10 9 8 7 6 5 4 3 2 1

Designed and produced for Godsfield Press by
The Bridgewater Book Company

Art Director: Sarah Howerd
Project Designer: Nicola Liddiard
Project Editor: Nicola Wright
Illustrator: Andrew Farmer

Printed and bound in China.

ISBN 1-84181-208-0

Contents

Apocraphya
Secret Writings

Apocryphal—"secret" or "hidden"

Apocrypha—Gnostic writings

Apocraphya—Secret Writings

1. *The word* pagan *is explained in the Anglican dictionary as "not acknowledging Jehovah, Christ, or Allah; non-Christian." However, the literal definition, adhered to by mystics, is derived from the original Latin,* paganus, *meaning "countryman," "delight in nature," "belief in nature gods and spirits," "the senses," and "polytheism of the ancient world."*

2. *Knowledge is Protection.*

3. *Protection is Power.*

KNOWLEDGE and PROTECTION are POWER. To thoroughly know something gives you protection. To be protected gives you power. To have power is to have knowledge and protection. The three are mutually beneficial. The more you can discover about areas of your individual interest, the more you increase your power. The protection instinct within us is a potent force that we are born with and that connects us to our earliest ancestors. We may not have the original memories of how to protect ourselves by producing fire from rubbing two sticks together, but we can certainly relearn those techniques, thereby regaining the original power. In these difficult and uncertain times, witches are not alone in needing essential skills of protection and survival. Whether it is a matter as complex as surviving your environment or as simple as protecting your day, the *Apocraphya* aims to bring you ideas and skills that will empower your life and show you that knowledge is protection is power!

Modern paranormal phenomena abound. Whether positive or negative, we have all at some time watched television shows, read letters to newspapers, and heard unexplained stories about the supernatural. There always seems to be someone who knows someone or something strange; however, the record of people who are deflecting negativity and realigning balance is less complete. In severe cases of concern, people often turn to the recognized Church. I and other like-minded people believe that many unexplained stories can be dealt with by individuals themselves. We have to let go of the idea that unexpected spiritual essence is negative. Oftentimes it is simply a strong energy that is trapped and needs to be released. Other times it is simply an energy that has tapped into a particularly sensitive individual and is trying to communicate. Still other times are when the spirit entity is trying to warn or guide someone.

The only thing we have to fear is fear itself. If we deal with all the different spirits in the same manner (rather like treating every ailment with an aspirin), it is not surprising that we come up against obstacles! Protection power is about recognizing individual energies and dealing with them specifically for a successful outcome to all concerned. Remember that no one has the right to encourage destruction or negativity in the name of religious or personal belief. There is no higher power that would condone such action and, if we are to follow the spiritual road, we must accept that negative action is not only self-defeating but also destroys our place in the cosmic hierarchy.

If you wish to learn some of the ancient skills of protection power and have the courage and belief necessary to practice them in this life, you will be constantly amazed and gratified by your results. Slowly, as you keep an open mind and start to increase your abilities, you will see that these gifts were meant for all of us, whether in times of deep trouble or simply as an aid to get through a stressful moment.

The Wiccan way is primarily about love and the many attributes that love encompasses, such as compassion, generosity, caring, and unselfishness.

With love as the overall tenet of pagan belief, you can do no wrong. Love does not deliberately wound others; it does not lie, cheat, or steal. Love saves your soul, for we are all essentially creatures of love. The Goddess of the Wiccan way is formed from three powers—Love, Light, and Life—and we as her children seek to emulate these three powers within us. Although we all hold the structure of the Goddess within us, our strong human element often draws us down or responds to our baser instincts. It is that human element that many of us fight against within ourselves and that can give rise to worldly problems. To aid us with these difficult facets of the human psyche, there are many protective and preservative laws within the magickal element from which we can all benefit. The Apocraphya is derived from hidden knowledge, with the ancient secret story of the cities of Cabal and N'Cabal (on pages 14, 46, and 96) briefly explaining the beginning of the pagan world, over 20,000 years ago. Part One of the Apocraphya covers the "Descriptive," and Part Two covers the "Active." These are followed in Part Three by the "Spells" from times past. The Descriptive section covers advice pertaining to your daily life and how you can protect yourself with knowledge. The Active section covers advice pertaining to how you can actually make things work for powerful protective results. So by the Knowledge and the Power you will have Pagan Protection for evermore.

As well as The Apocraphya, *the box contains other magickal items. Wear the Pentacle at any time to attract the forces of protection and* love. Use the Pouch to carry your pentacle or any amulet. The Sacred Scroll contains ancient mystical and powerful sigils and diagrams. Hang it in your home to protect your home and all who stay there. The Black Candle is used for spells and for connecting to the wise Crone aspect of the great Goddess.

There are many secrets hidden in the past and on the ether (upper regions of space), secrets that witches, druids, and pagans alike have long known about and held onto for the day that they may pass them on to others, safely and with love. We can all benefit from the wisdom of our pagan ancestors and the magick we hold deep within us. So I say to you: Simply believe, throw off suspicion and doubt, and be strong in your own Pagan Protection Power.

Brightest Blessings,

Gilly Sergiev

THE Story of Cabal

It was at the time of The Beginning, some 20,000 years past, when the very first mother city appeared, rising from the desert sands a veritable ship of glory—there where the Goddess Triformis stayed her ground—and the city was named Cabal. Cabal—the first city—she that appeared in the middle of a vast desert land where none had stood before.

This was the first time we lived together in peace and learned of our future destiny. Triformis made Cabal a place for her three emanations to stay and under whom we would thrive and prosper as her children—a race of people carrying her genes, attached to the great Mother Earth and, in symbiotic form, growing together. And it was in this same land that Triformis did indeed transmogrify into the three that were to stay: the first, Venus, Mistress of Cabal; the second, Flamen, Priestess of Cabal; and the third, Laetitia, Justiciar of Cabal. Under these three emanations Cabal stood firm, as secure and unwavering as though held within a gentle iron fist. The light circulated and peaceful trade and communication were the order of the day so life was good and spiritual awareness prospered. We, the people, grew strong and content and moved out across the Earth, beginning new habitats elsewhere as it was so intended, yet our ancestors remain at Cabal.

Stop now! I see time fly past, like a beautiful wraith in a trailing gown. Life's tender moments no longer pearl drops in a glass— now hurried, watchful, grasping at strings. Time flies past in too much of a hurry to stop for a moment and make discourse. Venus is attacked, Flamen is overwhelmed, and Laetitia is struck down. Where once was happy trade now sits a Goblin of darkness, pinching at the innocence and beliefs of others. Cabal is falling and the three emanations can only watch with an impending feeling of despair as their gift to humanity is destroyed by their very own children. Cabal is gone now, razed to the ground while the descendents of Triformis are pushed backward into the shade.

They remain hidden while a new Power rises. He sits upon the throne and his name is War. He names the new city N'Cabal, reflecting its rise from the ashes as a masculine power, a machine that takes what it wants and more, and so ignores its gentle children. The three female powers hide in the shadows and can only watch and wait. . .

PART ONE
Magickal Meanings

Descriptive

HE WAY OF THESE TEN *descriptions is this: To empower you with the knowledge of their powerful ability to create magick. Each description briefly covers the essence of the magickal intent therein, so that as* you become aware of its nature, so too can you develop your own connection with it and fly forwards into actively bringing alive that magick. These descriptions are intended as keys to doors that unlock the knowledge. When you enter a room, it is up to you where you go or what you do there. If you find for example that you are drawn to the essence of magick squares, follow your instincts and explore that room. Find out all there is to know so that properly empowered, when you create your own magick squares or work with existing ones you will be powerful indeed. Here, I have suggested ten of the more traditional descriptions of magickal ability that all witches should be comfortable

with, as a base for their ever-growing knowledge. Knowledge of these ten major protective areas will provide you with a secure base from where to practice your skills. Read the Omens, Create your Pentacle, Draw up a Magick Square, Shelter in the Eye of Horus, See through your Third Eye, Respect a Taboo, Listen to a Fetch, Whistle up the Wind, Enjoy a Trance, and Follow your Destiny. Do all these things and you will discover that you have learned the basis of how to fly. And as your soul lifts and your spirit soars, you will be guided and protected by your own doing, as well as by the magickal world that wishes you success.

1. Omen

HAPPENING OR THING PORTENDING GOOD OR
BAD PROPHETIC SIGNIFICANCE; INDICATION;
PREMONITION; SIGN

The *omen* is a forewarning of coming events and, whether as a sign of opportunity or a portent of danger, it is a mystical pointer on the path of life that we can all access for our own good.

Omens can be seen in everything that is out of the ordinary. Typical examples of omens can be found in the skies as shooting stars, rainbows, strange weather, and comets. Unexpected bird behavior, such as an owl hooting in the daytime, was a well-known omen in the past. Birds have always been regarded as the messengers between the two worlds and their behavior is often studied for coming portents of doom or glory. Animals and nature also hold powerful omen significance.

The black cat and the hare are both widely recognized as omens that a witch is in the area. Inanimate objects are also well-known as omens; most people have heard about the clock that stops just before a person dies, symbolizing the stopping of the person's life breath and showing the correlation between the time of the clock and the life span of a person. Breaking a mirror is an omen that portends seven years bad luck, while smashing a drinking glass indicates the coming of good fortune. We can find omens occurring regularly within ourselves as well, such as an itching left hand indicating money going out and an itching right hand indicating money coming in. When someone sneezes we automatically respond with "Bless you," thereby protecting the sneezer from whatever illness may be indicated. Even unexpected shivers on the body are associated with the saying; "Someone has walked over my grave."

The interpretation of omens is known as *augury* and was widely practiced in Roman times. Augury was the interpretation of coming events as messages from the Otherworld.

There were two types of augury, known as:

i. *Domestic Augury*, performed by the householder in private and dealing mainly with unexpected omens; and

ii. *Public Augury*, performed by college-trained augurs who advised public and military figures and dealing mainly with expected omens.

Unexpected omens were those that occurred by chance, such as breaking glass, sneezing, stumbling, and so on. These omens happened constantly and to such

a large extent that eventually they became so commonplace that their efficiency was undermined and less regarded by those in high positions, although remaining popular with the everyday people of the empire.

Expected omens, however, were more highly regarded and occurred when the augurs were particularly looking for them to happen. These omens included comets in the sky, particular patterns in the weather, and the individual calls and flight patterns of birds. These omens were valued by the higher officials, particularly before making important national decisions. Visions have always been considered powerful omens and many a battle was won with the knowledge of a predetermined successful outcome in the victor's mind.

A favorite form of augury in Roman times was performed using sacred chickens as messengers of the omen. Letters of the alphabet were placed in a circle with a grain of corn or wheat placed upon each one. The chicken, representing chance or the messenger, was placed in the middle of the circle and then allowed to eat the grains. The letters revealed once the grain was eaten were considered chosen specifically by the messenger and then interpreted into words and answers to the situation at hand.

At the Tower of London, the wings of the ravens are regularly clipped to prevent the birds from flying away. The omen foretells that if the ravens ever desert the Tower, the city of London will be in ruins. It is interesting to note that despite our ever-increasing knowledge and scientific discovery, omens are still highly regarded and respected by modern-day folk.

OMEN means ‹   a Sign from the Moon.

OSTENTA means ‹   an Omen that makes clear.

PORTENTA means ‹   an Omen that foreshadows.

MONSTRA means ‹   an Omen that demonstrates.

PRODIGIA means ‹   an Omen that gives a sign through a miracle.

2. Mandala & Pentacle

MANDALA ‑ SANSKRIT FOR "CIRCLE" ‑ A SYMBOLIC FIGURE

USED IN MAGICK AND CONTAINED WITHIN A CIRCLE

Even though the similarities between a *mandala* and a *pentacle* are pronounced (both are mystical circles that can be physically depicted or mentally invoked) their individual qualities represent quite specific and different purposes for magickal ceremony.

The mandala is a beautifully formed and illustrated circle using any medium, including mental imagery, depicted within a square or four points, which encloses and contains the power of the deity or image depicted within it. By magickal ritual, the deity is invited into the circle and contained there for the duration of the spellwork. Once the deity has been invoked within the circle, the mandala becomes known as a *yantra*, which means it has become a device of forceful energy. Each yantra is individualized depending on the characteristics of the deity or image housed within. The designs of the mandala vary as to their specific purpose and power; however, they can be constructed with mathematical precision when effecting magick concerned with numerology or maze work. Other times they may unexpectedly take on a specific life of their own from their design, becoming a healing enclosure, meditational circle, or a good fortune talisman. In the construction of the mandala as a circle placed within a square, the square symbolizes the four cardinal points, the circle is the 'Golden Flower' of light, and contained within and about these two main images are many and varied sigils (symbols) concerned with the particular magickal power connecting you with the mandala. Creating a mandala and giving it life is something that should only be attempted after careful study of the properties, background, and history of mandalas, so that you become fully aware of its function and treat the ritual with respect and proper understanding. Be aware that the mandala can be used for negative purposes as well as positive and that is why you should only attempt to use a mandala when you thoroughly understand its life force and purpose. There are some beautiful examples of mandalas painted on temple walls in Tibet, but your first step in this direction should be to visit a library or bookshop that can provide you with specialized knowledge on this subject. The circle's boundary represents our infinite life and to enter it becomes a journey to find the soul.

PENTACLE ⁓ A SYMBOLIC PENTAGRAM USED IN MAGICK
AND CONTAINED WITHIN A CIRCLE

Unlike the mandala, whose image within the circle differs depending on its use, a pentacle is always a five-pointed star (pentagram) within a circle. The five points denote the four elements of air, fire, water, and earth plus the sacred element of spirit. The circle is the boundary within which the magick is protected and contained. It may be considered a fixed mandala and is a powerful protective image used specifically for the purpose of protecting the spellworker, an object contained within it, or whoever invokes it in the name of protection power.

Pentacles can be constructed in any size and from any matter. They are used both as amulets and talismans that can be embroidered or painted on clothing, tattooed on the body, or made into items of jewelry. Or they can stand apart as statues, engravings, or images within your home as a constant protective force.

It is essential to stand within a pentacle when performing magick such as "Drawing down the Moon" so that, as you connect with the Goddess you do so in a contained space of power and protection, untouched by anything around you other than the magick that you are performing. No matter what the situation, to touch a pentacle in moments of need is to connect with a positive and protective energy. If you invoke a pentacle within your mind's eye, it should be imagined as a blazing figure of light, for as you concentrate on its awesome beauty and power, you will actually be connecting with and becoming part of that all-loving and protective spirit or Golden Flower around us and inside us.

3. Magick *Square*

NUMBERS, LETTERS, OR IMAGES

ARRANGED IN A SQUARE SHAPE

FOR MAGICKAL PURPOSE

Powerful magick can be obtained through careful manipulation of numbers, images, or letters of the alphabet that are arranged in a square shape. Numbers are believed by mystics to be the basis of the essential structure of the Universe, images are a powerful form of *sigil* (occult symbol) display, and names are believed to hold the vital essence of a person or thing. Therefore, by combining these three major principals of magickal theory, you can create a magick square to contain all of these powers.

Squares based on the planets are widely known, but as a neophyte interested in this form of magick, you will be able to create your own powerful squares for yourself. When using numbers for a magick square, they should appear in the square only once. The idea is for all the numbers to add up to the same total when read either diagonally, vertically, or horizontally. If you can create this balanced totality you have started with the first magickal force in your square. Saturn, for example, is made up of three rows of three, containing the numbers 4, 9, 2, then 3, 5, 7, then 8, 1, 6. The sum of this square equals 15 and is said to bring good luck and protection from ill fortune. Jupiter, on the other hand, is made up of four rows of four, containing the following numbers: 4, 14, 15, 1; then 9, 7, 6, 12; then 5, 11, 10, 8; then 16, 2, 3, 13. The sum of this square equals 34. The square for the Sun adds up to 111 and brings good fortune and success to the holder. Mars adds up to 65, Venus adds up to 175, Mercury adds up to 260, the Moon adds up to 369, and so forth.

Magick squares may also be made from images and letters of the alphabet, spelling out sacred or magickal words and names. Again, they should read the same diagonally, horizontally, or vertically. For example, the SATOR magick square is made up of five individual sacred names of five letters each, which are listed as follows: SATOR, then AREPO beneath it, then TENET beneath that, then OPERA under that, and finally, ROTAS at the bottom. This is an ancient square found, among other places, in the ruins of a Roman villa near Cirencester. It is a protective magick square and believed to be particularly effective as a fire deterrent! Another well-known square, again five words of five letters each, is the MILON, which is made up of the names MILON, followed by IRAGO, then LAMAL, then OGARI, and finally NOLIM. By carrying this square on your person you are believed to attract the gift of prophesy. Another magickal word, AGLA, makes its own magickal square in a slightly different way by simply repeating in a circular movement the word AGLA. This is a talismanic square used for good fortune; the initials of the word AGLA are believed by some to stand for Aleth, Gadol, Leolam, and Adonai, meaning, "Thou art mighty forever, O God."

4. Eye *of* Horus

A MYSTICAL PROTECTIVE SYMBOL

CREATING NEW LIFE

Since earliest times, the depiction of an eye as a magickal symbol has been found the world over. Primarily it represents the all-seeing eye of the Creator as a protective force, but depending on its color, angle of view, depiction, or position, its magickal properties can differ. The eye of Horus is based in the Egyptian religion and is also known as an Uzat or Udjat—an amulet that is worn to encourage the attributes of the Sun God's power—health, wealth, and long life—onto the wearer.

The story concerning the eye of Horus explains that when his evil brother Seth tore Horus' eye out, Horus took it to his dead father Osiris. When Osiris received the eye of Horus, he became a soul and was renewed in the Otherworld, where he would live forever. Thus this sigil became a powerful ritualistic amulet that each Egyptian son presented at the funeral of his father. It was engraved on coffins or placed within the funerary wrappings. The sigil became more frequently associated with keeping watch and protecting the person from harm as well as guaranteeing eternal life to the wearer. The classic depiction of two eyes, side by side, was derived from this sigil. The eyes were believed to be the eye of the Moon (left) and the eye of the Sun (right), which gave total protection and power

to the wearer or area where they were depicted. The Eye Temple of Brak, dating from 3000 B.C.E. and situated in Tell Brak in Mesopotamia, contained literally thousands of statues whose only identifiable feature was a pair of enlarged eyes. Whether shown vertically or horizontally on the statue, it was clear that the eyes themselves were of prime importance and that they contained the magickal essence. The image was believed to be that of the Mother Goddess whose all-seeing power was the protective force. This symbol has been found all over the world, primarily in the Megalithic cultures of Cyprus, Crete, Greece, Malta, Sicily, Italy, Spain, France, Britain, and Ireland. The Eye of Horus explains itself in the Coffin Texts as follows: "I am the all-seeing Eye of Horus, whose appearance strikes terror, Lady of Slaughter, Mighty One of Frightfulness," also indicating the powerful feminine Goddess attributed to Hathor.

So in totality, it is suggested that the Eye of Horus should be depicted twice as if in a mirror image: the one on the left indicating the feminine power of Hathor (or the Moon), Creation, protection, and the reduction of negativity; and the one on the right indicating the masculine power of Horus (or the Sun), reincarnation, and eternal life. In this way you can recreate a powerful form of protective magick to either use in your home or wear upon your person.

5. The *Third* Eye

INVISIBLE AND MYSTICAL EYE,

OPERATOR OF GREAT MAGICK

The third eye that mystics refer to is situated between the eyebrows and about one half inch higher on the forehead. This eye refers to hidden powers such as the resting place of the Golden Flower Light; second sight; clairvoyancy; or supernatural vision. The third eye of the god Shiva is believed to be so powerful as to create or destroy a universe.

The third eye of each and every one of us remains hidden, yet can be a powerful channel of magick should we choose to use it. The normal eyes of a person are thought to be the windows of the soul through which the spiritual light (the Golden Flower) can be seen, able to create certain magick by manipulation in their own right; however, accessing the third eye ability takes a person one step further in magickal understanding, for this is the seat of the Golden Flower light. The power of the third eye can scry (divine) images in crystal balls and mirrors or view events on the astral plane. The third eye often comes into play when we dream particularly strong or relevant visions. To seek with the third eye is to gaze upon secrets not normally seen.

The light contained within the third eye, through the magick of mediation, makes itself into a spirit body or etheric (spirit) double so that it can move outside the conscious body. If the light goes out within the conscious body, that body dies; however, if the light is transferred to the etheric double, the spiritual life will continue forever. The idea is to move the light from the conscious body into the spirit body so that it can never go out. The human body will eventually die, but if you have created a spirit body for the light to move into, your essence will never die. Nowadays it is fashionable for people to wear glittering, colored "Bindi" (small drops, circles, or star-shaped patches) in the area of the third eye, similar to the red, white, or yellow spots Hindi women traditionally wear there. By doing so, whether intentionally or unintentionally, you are drawing attention to an ancient and mystical power that you hold within yourself and hopefully, will one day access for positive results.

6. Taboo & Geas

TABOO ⁄ A BAN OR RULE IN SOCIETY, OFTEN RELIGIOUS,

THE BREAKING OF WHICH RESULTS IN MISFORTUNE.

FROM THE POLYNESIAN *TABU*.

Taboos are restrictive or essential rules that ensure good fortune when followed or completed successfully. Any taboo when viewed separately may appear irrational and it is only when viewed within the context of the surrounding society or belief system that it begins to make sense.

Every culture contains a complex group of values, belief systems, and rules that holds it together as a group. To break a taboo within that system is to break the cultural strength itself. Therefore, a taboo has a certain element of control over a social system and keeping the taboo correctly is symbolic of keeping the culture

strong. A simple example of modern-day taboo is the hygienic restriction of keeping the bathroom and kitchen apart. You would not think of putting them together due to the risk of transference of germs from the toilet to the food supply. To break this simple taboo could have unhealthy results.

GEAS ✦ A BOND, SPELL, OR MAGICKAL TABOO, THE BREAKING

OF WHICH RESULTS IN MISFORTUNE.

FROM THE IRISH *GEIS*.

The geas is a mystical example of the common taboo. It is intended as a means of correct behavior toward the Fairy World since keeping the sacred obligations ensures the continuance of good magickal energy between the two worlds. Like the taboo, the geas was a prohibition, restriction, or essential rule and expected to be followed exactly.

Some people are born with a geas and some people have geasa thrust upon them, as did the Irish noble, Conary, whose totem was a bird. Conary's true father was the bird, Danaan, from the Fairy World; therefore, his geas was that he was not allowed to kill birds. After Conary became King, seven more geasa were applied to him. The breaking of these eight geasa resulted in Conary's demise. The geas can be broken unintentionally and without the person's knowledge; however, the taboo is so strong that misfortune will almost always follow as a result. Another great Celtic hero was Cuchulainn, the guardian of Ulster, who as a boy killed a hound belonging to a smith called Culainn and as a result received the name; "the Hound of Culainn." As recompense for his act, Cuchulainn promised to protect Culainn but forever after the dog was a taboo animal to Cuchulainn. Unfortunately, entities from the Otherworld trapped Cuchulainn and made him break his geas by eating a meal of roast dog, thereby ensuring his downfall.

7. The *Fetch*

PSYCHIC DOUBLE OF A PERSON FOREWARNING
ILL HEALTH OR IMPENDING DEATH

Also known as a wraith, the fetch is the spectral appearance of a still-living person, believed to portend that person's death. It is known that some people have an awareness or premonition of their death and often settle their affairs before dying. Based on this knowledge, the fetch image is an intense physical extension of this understanding that a person may unconsciously send to someone close through the desire to communicate before they pass over, to convey a message, or even to settle a score before passing on to the Otherworld.

The fetch is best described as a visible representation of a person's soul, known as an etheric double, for the purpose of visiting the astral plane, warning someone at risk, or working a positive spell.

Depictions of etheric doubles can be found in paintings that show a person's aura (the aureole of light that surrounds the whole body), halo (the nimbus that surrounds the head only), or shadow, such as is seen in the famous and stunning painting by Rosetti, entitled, "How they Met Themselves," which clearly portrays two people viewing their doppelgangers. These etheric bodies are also sometimes caught on camera in ghostly form or more clearly as in Kilner's auric photographs. In the case of the fetch, it is believed that the doppelganger or spirit double can exist quite separately from its host, but to view your own fetch is usually an omen of impending death.

At the time of Samhain (Halloween) there is an ancient custom whereby if you hide near a church porch at midnight, you may see a procession of fetches pass by, indicating the actual people in that parish who are destined to pass over soon. However, there is always the possibility that you might see your own fetch, so this practice is not to be encouraged. In the case of the well-known folk-tale, a local man saw a fairy funeral pass by one Samhain and, peering into the coffin the fairies were carrying, he was horrified to see his own appearance lying there. The tale reveals that after telling his neighbors about his ghastly experience, he was found the following day having expired in his bed with no obvious cause of death.

In the case of one's own fetch, it is more commonly an apparition that appears to someone they feel strongly about. There seems to be a psychic energy that projects its thought form through the intensity of emotion, enabling the fetch to communicate one last time. Leaving a loved one is a difficult thing to do at the best of times, but the intensity of emotion from knowing that you are about to pass over can quite easily be explained as the force that projects the fetch. It is said by some that if a fetch is seen before noon, the passing over is not immediate; this sending would be useful for anyone who had to travel, giving them enough time to visit their dying friend. Alternatively, if a fetch is seen after noon, then the moment of passing over is believed to be fairly imminent.

In Celtic tales particularly, there are anecdotes of people seeing their own fetch and refusing to accept the symbolism, and who are then pursued or haunted by the fetch until a magickal solution presents itself or the hero meets his untimely end. Queen Elizabeth the First of England was reported to have viewed her fetch while on her deathbed and was shocked to see herself looking so "pallid and shriveled." Catherine the Great of Russia is also said to have seen her fetch

appear before her—and ordered her guards to shoot it!

There is an ancient custom of hanging a black cloth over all the mirrors in the house when a person passes over. This custom originated in the belief that the reflections of the living people in the house could be captured by the departing fetch and taken with them, causing their death as well. If you accidentally view your own fetch, the best advice I can think of is to shut your eyes and conjure up the image of the pentacle. Make it swing widdershins (counterclockwise) in your mind's eye, bathing you in a glowing and healing light as it does so. If you view a fetch of someone close to you, I advise you to hurry to his side.

8. Whistling Up
The Wind

A FORM OF SPELLWORK USED BY WITCHES

AND CONNECTED TO THE FOUR ELEMENTS

To whistle up the wind is a form of spellwork commonly accredited to witches. There are several ways to perform this magick and several reasons why one would want to do so. If a fisherman, for example, wanted to increase his catch, he might pay a witch to gently stir the seas and encourage the fish into his net. On the other hand, powerful seafaring warriors might apply to a witch to cause a storm at sea by whistling up gales, thereby giving them power over their enemies

There are two main ways of whistling up the wind:

i. The first concerns the gently sympathetic magick of whistling and knot work, which attracts and copies the movement and flow of the wind. The strength and length of the whistling duplicating the corresponding wind power, and the knot work ritually untied, increases the power of the wind as this is done. This spell

is nearly always performed standing at the edge of the sea where the dual natures
of the Wind (Air) and Sea (Water) connect with the witch's energy to produce
a positive result.

ii. The second way of whistling up the wind concerns a stronger type of
sympathetic magick wherein symbolism is the order of the day. The witch uses
eggshells as an Earth tool, representing boats, to connect with the energy of Fire in
a bonfire or fireplace; by throwing them into the fire a certain way and chanting
certain magickal words, she can encourage the dual natures of the hearth (Fire)
and the eggshells (Earth) to connect with her energy, producing powerful results
where required.

9. Trance

A STATE WHEREIN THE CONSCIOUS ACCESSES THE UNCONSCIOUS
AND IN DOING SO ENTERS ANOTHER DIMENSION

In order to effect a successful trance you must first be in a positive mental state. When you are in a trance, every nuance of every moment is heightened and affected by your mood, so for your own protection it is essential that your outlook is positive. A trance is performed to access a different state of mind and from that state enjoy a new journey of discovery encompassing a completely separate dimension of reality.

A trance has been explained as the soul separating from the body, extreme ecstasy, or rapture. If the soul does leave the body at the moment of trance, it makes sense that the empty body can be used as a channel for spiritual advice and communication. This is why mediums and channelers first enter a trance in order to communicate with spirits from the Otherworld. In many cultures the person who enacts this ritual and goes into a trance is known as an oracle. The most famous of these oracles is the Oracle of Delphi in ancient Greece, which was not only consulted by local citizens but was also visited by people from all over the world.

There are various ways to enter a trance and in the ancient times certain drugs, incense, chanting, drumming, music, and even dancing rituals were regularly used. Their desired effect was to render the trancee into a state of unusual and altered mental intoxication whereby he could then access the required alternative dimension.

Sometimes the oracle or trancee becomes a channel for the spirits, and other times he literally becomes the actual spirit or god. In the majority of cases, the person can usually remember nothing after the throes of a trance. This is because her conscious form is apart from her physical form, so no record of her actions can be easily stored.

When trance is practiced with intense belief, the practitioner may be able to physically alter or change his appearance in some way. In the case of a certain Mr. Galton, a famous physiologist of the past, he is said to have concentrated on becoming the most hated man in the world, after which he recorded a variety of unpleasant reactions from people around him. I would say that he erred in his desire to be despised. He deliberately encouraged a negative state and reaction in others, which is a highly dubious form of trance exploration. He and his associates would no doubt have benefited more by concentrating on love. Other semi-trance states can be achieved while conscious. These are magickal rituals of invocation such as drawing down the moon or rapture trances whereby the trancee

retains a certain amount of consciousness while in an otherwise altered state.

The essential purpose of an entranced state is to access an alternative state through the power of meditational skills, for the purpose of communication and magickal or spiritual understanding.

10. Destiny

POWER THAT FOREORDAINS (PREDESTINES)
THE LOT (FATE) OF A PERSON OR THE COURSE OF EVENTS

The physical explanation of destiny can be found in the unique set of genes that we are all born with. Within each strand of DNA that makes up your genes is the reflection of a set destiny, pre-programmed at birth. In a sense it is your life-plan of how things could be, should you so desire. Your future is initially predestined in a certain way by your genes. For example, some genes may be predisposed to certain illnesses, while other genes are responsible for particular characteristics and talents. Knowing this, it is natural for us to sit back and ask why we should make any effort at all in life, if our destiny is already pre-programmed. After all, what difference would any of our efforts make to our lives if the final destiny is already set? The answer to the age-old question is the second gift we are given, the gift called fate.

Fate

Fate is a random occurrence, not unlike unexpected weather, which drops in and out of our pre-set destiny, often inflicting tremendous life changes. Fate is neither wholly positive nor wholly negative. It is random and falls how it may. With the unexpected visits of fate throughout our life journey we can never be totally sure of our destiny. Fate is the unexpected bombshell that throws us off course. Perhaps

best of all is the third gift we are given, the gift that is called free will.

Free Will

We all have the power within ourselves to change our own destiny and fate's bombshells. The soul within us is the physical holder of that free will, so even though we may be programmed on a set course by our genetic destiny, our essential soul lets us influence and change this destiny and fate if we truly so wish. Therein lies the crux of the matter: do we truly wish it?

In order to change our destiny or gene determination, we have to work extremely hard to reprogram or relearn our mystic roots and apply them to a new way of thinking. We must take charge ourselves of where our futures will lie and in which direction we choose to go. To each of us is given that third gift of free will to determine who we really want to be. It allows us, through perseverance, to empower the original set of genes given at birth, to alter our destiny, and to create new, enhanced genes which are then passed on to the next new sparks of life.

Of course many people are happy to sit back and accept destiny and the random flux that fate throws at them. To those people will come the simple determination of destiny charged at their birth—nothing more, nothing less.

But to those who recognize the limitations of their destiny and unconscious fate, who seek to grow and enhance their own possibilities through the power of free will, to them will come all that they wish for.

To try to understand the nature of that one guiding spiritual essence that inspires all this, we can look briefly at the mechanics of quantum physics for some answers. I am no expert on quantum physics but the way I see it is as follows:

If we can first agree that there is no such thing as nothing, that even nothing contains something (for "nothing" actually contains zillions of particles of quantum nature "something"), then we can say that the random flux of quantum energy that preceded the Big Bang was the essence of the Great Goddess roaming the void before she made the null (i.e., the Big Bang). When we apply this thought to the Big Bang theory, we can simply say that in the beginning was a quantum nature energy that we know as the Great Goddess and that the void before the Big Bang contained the Goddess's nature in its entirety.

It is agreed by most scientists that the values of this universe are very finely tuned in order for life to survive. It is also said there must be a designer behind the universe. This is known as the specific value arising from the logical theory. Therefore, I believe that the designer is the Great Goddess.

Some believe that this is not the only universe, that there are trillions of them with their constants having all sorts of values. Our constants are such that they allow us to evolve as human beings. In another universe the laws of nature may be entirely different from ours, resulting in a completely different constant. All these constants, however, are still ultimately fixed to enable matter to develop. Our cosmological constant is a ridiculously tiny number such as 10 to the power of minus 120. Taking this into consideration, it is obvious that we haven't even begun to understand what we are truly capable of as human beings. All these constants are set by the Great Goddess for a purpose (the law of quantum mechanics). She is in everyone and in everything. The ultimate reality is the Great Goddess.

The proof of this has to be found and experienced by each and every one of us through free will by individually touching the Goddess within us and through that act individually experiencing the Truth. Scientists say that the universe is defined by our presence in it. Therefore, I say that as the Goddess is within us (and we are in the Goddess), the Goddess herself defines the universe.

By accepting this logical and quantum way of thinking, we have chosen through our free will to challenge the preconceptions of the Big Bang theory or other creation theories and have subtly changed our own destiny. Instead of accepting a preconceived value, we have now challenged it and accepted something else. By doing so we are now walking down a different road. By walking down that uncertain road, guided by our spiritual friends, we are all taking the first steps towards a vibrant and positive future where we will all ultimately be free to decide who it is that we truly wish to be.

THE Story *of* N'Cabal

The first city of peace, Cabal, has been destroyed by the ruler named War, our Ancestors gone. He has rebuilt our ancient city and calls it N'Cabal, a place that exists without peace or compassion. N'Cabal is primed and waiting to fight. War strides across his land, ebullient in nature. That first sacred moment of quiet is now lost forever. It will take five millennia before Triformis returns to claim her ground and, in the meantime, War rages and spits from his throne in N'Cabal at all the new cities across the world. The people are thin and tired now, and the twins, Disease and Despair, are great friends of War. They follow him everywhere, leaving a trail of destruction. Venus, Flamen, and Laetitia watch from some hidden place, offering support to those that seek them out, but understanding that their strength comes from retreat at this time. There are ways to fight War, but they are not easily accomplished and demand much understanding. Those of us who persevere keep hold of time's delicate golden chains. We know that our season will come again. Now is the time of the conscious heart, containing the light of the Golden Flower, unable to move. We all know that for the dormant and peace-loving Cabal to rise again and to embrace the moving force that is War, it will take great love and some magick. So, slowly and in secret places, we hold fast to the wisdom in the pearls of time and wait, hiding the golden light. War laughs triumphantly, glorifying in his prowess, for he cannot see what is to come. He is simply the fool waiting to fall.

PART TWO
Magickal Tools & Practices

Active

NDERSTANDING THE THEORY *of a thing, as we all know, is only half the battle. We cannot fully appreciate a chocolate log Yule cake by simply reading the recipe— we have to make one and taste it for ourselves. This segment of ten activities is for you to quickly practice and thereby come to fully taste their properties. With the knowledge of "how" you must now attempt to "do": you have read the recipes, now taste the cake. These ten active magicks are more geared towards immediate magickal work. So by using a sigil, amulet, or ingredient, for example, you are bringing it alive by the mere process of touching it. Of course it is important to understand the description behind these ten active components, but they are chosen for the powerful magick simply behind their very nature. For example, a magick square from the previous set demands a detailed description and understanding of how it will work for you.*

A sigil from the active set of ten, however, will work the minute you draw it and call its name, whether or not you understand its composition. Of course, you must always be fully aware of the magick you are creating, but I have attempted to offer ten active magicks that can be quickly understood for immediate use. If you need an ingredient for a protective spell, it is not immediately necessary to know all about the history or whereabouts of that ingredient before you use it. Naturally, if you choose to concentrate your talents on protective spellwork, you will almost certainly in time come to be an expert on the wherewithal of ingredients. At this point, however, I hope these ten active magicks will kick-start your power and get you flying higher than ever.

1. Sigil

MAGICKAL SIGN OR MARK

SYMBOLIZING A THING OR FORCE

A sigil is a powerful image used mostly for protective reasons, healing, attracting wealth and power, and communicating with the Otherworld. The Sigil—through its image, shape, color, size, and depiction—functions as a magickal figure that will interact with the forces of the Universe. It enables matter and energy to combine to produce a supernatural effect such as protection, communication, or fortune. A glyph is one type of sigil; it is a graphic representation in astrology, related primarily to the signs of the zodiac and planets.

By combining particular elements of magickal knowledge into an object form, the witch or mystic creates a sigil for a particular purpose. Many well-known sigils are copied and used just as effectively. They include simple forms such as circles, triangles, crosses, and squares as well as more detailed forms such as the pentacle or Eye of Horus. Mandalas, magick squares and runic imagery represent even more intricate sigils. By understanding the potency of numbers, colors, and words, mystics are able to create their own sigils and thereby cause their unique magick to evolve.

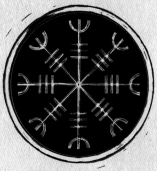

By representing certain aspects of magick in pictorial form, the mystic brings power to that image through esoteric knowledge and, by invoking that power, releases the magick for positive effect. The more understanding you have of occult (magickal) secrets, the better you are able to create a powerful sigil.

The ancient Egyptians believed that by knowing someone's true name, they would have power over that person. Similarly, knowledge of the elements that make up a sigil gives mystics the power to invoke the sigil's magick.

For protective purposes, the most powerful sigil for a witch is the pentacle, a pentagram (five-pointed star) within a circle. The pentagram calls upon the aid of the four elements and the one spirit. By containing it within a circle you are metaphorically surrounding yourself with protection from the entire universe. By wearing this sigil, having it nearby, or even standing within a depiction of the sigil, you are ensuring profound otherworldly protection. If you want to help people, there is no better way than to mentally send this sigil to them.

2. Ingredients

COMPONENTS OF A MIXTURE

Ingredients are the components of something. In spellwork the ingredients are items that hold magickal energies, secret symbolism, and references to the Otherworld. Knowing the magickal components can help you determine the exact and specific direction of your spellwork. Ingredients can come from anywhere and the more you research the energies and symbolism of things, the better you can decide their usage as ingredients for your own magickal work.

General ingredients in witchcraft are taken from nature. They may include herbs, plants, trees, water, oils, foodstuffs, spices, salts, wax, crystals, stones, earth, and feathers. These items are combined or used in a variety of magickal ways in rituals, potions, and chants to release their energies and work for the positive outcome of your spellwork. Specific ingredients such as strands of hair, nail clippings, saliva, pieces of clothing, statues, images, and so forth are used in particular spells for the good of a person by sympathetic magick.

Ingredients are the physical representation of the spellwork being performed and every witch determines which particular ingredients work best. Below are a few basic and well-known ingredients that can be easily found, along with their magickal properties:

EGG	New beginnings, health, luck, new life, transportation, the Maid aspect
ROSE	Fertility, love, luck, midlife, attraction, the Mother aspect
APPLE	Wisdom, love, psychic powers, long life, health, the Crone aspect
TOMATO	Wealth, protection, lust
BAY LEAF	Protection, psychic healing, wishes, purification
NETTLE	Removing curses, protection, fertility, exorcism
PINE	Cleansing, money, fertility
THISTLE	Exorcism, healing, removing hexes
BLACKBERRY	Healing, money, protection, banishing
GARLIC	Protection, removing hexes, healing, weather, absorption, exorcism
NUTS	Wealth, fertility, good fortune, health
OAK LEAVES	Fertility, luck, money, protection, strength, male issues, the Consort aspect
PARSLEY	Purification, lust, fertility, protection
ROWAN (MOUNTAIN ASH) BARK	Psychic ability, healing, success, wealth, protection, power
MISTLETOE	Healing, removing hexes, protection, love, fertility
MINT	Travel, purification, protection, money, exorcism
LEMON	Cleansing, purification, friendship, long life
IVY	Female strength, protection, love, healing, fairies, scrying
HOLLY	Dreams, protection, good luck, feminine issues, the Goddess aspect
MUSHROOMS	Prophecy, healing, protection, psychic ability
HAIR	Binding, healing, prophecy
SILVER	Goddess calling, wealth, success, the Moon aspect
GOLD	God calling, health, strength, the Sun aspect
PINS	Protection, hex breaking, hiding, judgments
OIL	Scrying, prophecy, spellworking
SALT	Purification, cleansing, spirit calling
STONES	Healing, wishes, spirit calling, Earth power
WATER	Purification, healing, scrying, power, dispersal

3. Amulet

FROM THE LATIN *AMULETUM* ⁄ A PROTECTIVE OBJECT

THAT REPELS GENERAL NEGATIVITY FROM A THING OR PERSON

An amulet's function is to project power in an outward movement, thereby repelling any negative influence from the bearer. Amulets are traditionally worn as jewelry in the form of brooches, necklaces, rings, or bracelets, or carried about the person in pockets, hats, or shoes as a symbolic protective force akin to a magickal shield or visor. Often rare items, amulets are usually found in their natural state. Particular stones include hag stones, which have naturally occurring holes in them, and amber resin. The amulet may contain unusual colors or shapes, or a lucky item like a four-leaf clover, a horseshoe, garlic, a star sapphire, or gemstones such as emerald, coral, opal, garnet, and jet. However, they can also be made and charmed in ritual ways, such as empowering them with magickal sigils and hanging them around the body. As a general protective charm, however, an amulet works best when used in its natural state.

The ancient Egyptians were very fond of amulets and there are numerous examples such as scarabs, the head of Bes, the Ankh, the Tedjet, and so on. In other cultures there are many different items used both for amuletic and talismanic magick. Well-known items include the African gris-gris, an amulet to ward off evil, images from the Chinese I Ching or Shu Ching ancient texts, Arabic verses from the Koran, relics, and divine names of God. Maoris use an image made from jade called the Hei-tiki, and Zoroastrans use a special woven shirt. The Tau Cross is an amuletic image that corresponds to the last letter in the Hebrew alphabet and is shaped like the letter T. Because of its position within the Hebrew alphabet, it is often linked to the idea of the end of the world and therefore, by association, represents protection against evil.

If you are lucky enough to find an unusual or rare amulet you must first purify it with running water and pray or chant over it. By wearing or carrying it constantly, it will then take on your etheric (spiritual) force and grow in strength as your personal protective shield.

In both amulet and talisman usage, importance is placed on the attention and ritual devoted to an individual object. Over time its qualities will be enhanced through your enchanted magnetic charge.

4. Talisman

FROM THE GREEK *TELESMA* ⟩ A CHARMED OBJECT THAT ATTRACTS

PARTICULAR POSITIVITY TO A THING OR PERSON

A talisman's function is to ingest power in an inward movement, thereby attracting a positive influence toward oneself. Talismans are usually objects specifically made or used for good luck purposes and then ritually enchanted; they may include plaited wristbands, statues, scrolls, crystals, and cloths. Sometimes a talisman includes magickal sigils and is hung or positioned within the home. Talismans are traditionally positioned in a static place of importance as a defending force, like a magickal sword or guard dog.

To make a talisman you will need an object such as paper, material, metal, wood, or stone that is either new or purified with running water. Your Will and personal energy is then combined with magickal sigils and words to mystically saturate and permeate the object in question. Using the best quality papers, stones, or metals will ensure a high-quality and enduring talisman. By constantly referring to the magick, such as singing vibrational notes around it, using visualization imagery, or touching it, it will grow in power and protective quality. Traditionally, talismans are kept hidden in the home under a piece of black or dark blue cloth, or hung in an unseen corner of the house, so as not to disturb their protective psychic force by the unwanted gaze of others.

5. Charm

FROM THE LATIN *CARMEN* ∕ TO SING

A charm is a magickal spell that should be recited, sung, or chanted over an object, thus imbuing it with magickal properties to affect the desired result. To charm something brings good luck. Charm work is included in the making of talismans and amulets as part of the magickal process of bringing otherworldly power to the object. When an object has been charmed, it is then protected by the spellwork and invigorated into positive attraction for the benefit of the owner. Through the vibrational tones of song, chanting, or recitation, you use the power of your Will to penetrate the object and direct conscious magick throughout the item, bringing it alive in a positive and protective way. The combination of the vibrational tones used, magick words of power, mathematical positioning (placement of object), and effort of the will results in a powerful force that magnetizes the object. When one refers to having a lucky charm, one means that the object in question has been magickally "powered" to bring good fortune and deflect negativity.

People can be charmed in a certain way, but because of our individual spirit and will, this can only be a temporary situation and certainly not something to force upon another. When you listen to a particularly beautiful or powerful piece of music, you can be said to be charmed by it; this is a brief example of the similar change in nature that is affected by magickal charm work over objects. Take a stone, for example. It can be said to undergo a transformation of state similar to what you feel when you listen to a powerful piece of music or song. The stone undergoes a transformation that makes it comie alive with magickal properties. The power word ABRAXAS is often used in ritual charm work, paying attention to and concentrating your Will on the vibrational pull of each letter as it is sung.

6. Witch's *Payment*

ANCIENT LAW OF NATURE

Most neophytes, when starting their spellwork for others, often decline any form of payment, holding fast to the rule that "what goes around comes around" and knowing that helping others is an important tenet of the witch's life. That is all very good and commendable; however, there are some exceptions to this rule that are useful to understand. I and many like me have found that once you start spellworking for no charge, word gets around and suddenly that is all you seem to be doing, day in and day out. This would be fine if your days could be spent totally concentrating on helping others, but unfortunately most of us have other responsibilities to attend to. Another problem is that the witch can be exhausted with nonstop spellwork since each spell is performed by giving out a little of the witch herself. If this is overused, the witch can become tired or even ill. In extreme cases she may even become destitute since most ingredients for spell-work cost something and by constantly giving out and not receiving back the balance is severely upset. The emotional force that a witch uses in spellworking can exhaust even the most adept of adepts if not properly balanced.

There is yet another point to consider. The work that a witch does is honest, sacred, and for the good of another. If this value is not recognized by the other person via some form of return gift, it belittles the work itself. Respect each other's gifts and then you will be on the right wavelength. By requesting payment from a seeker, you will find out whether the person is genuinely interested or only in it for a laugh and therefore wasting your time.

The witch's payment is considered a rightful gift to give in exchange for the gift of a magick or spell. Thus all is balanced between the two and no one is another's debt. In medieval times, common witch payments depended on how well off the seeker was and usually consisted of a favor in return; for example, a chicken or some silver coins. Nowadays, a witch's payment should be of equal value to the service provided, whether in terms of money or an actual item that the witch requests. Alternatively, if as a witch you cannot bring yourself to name an item or figure, you can always leave it to the other person to give what they feel the work is worth. Whatever you decide, it is important to realize that your work is special, and if someone wishes to benefit from your gift, it is only right and proper that they recompense you accordingly. In this way, equal respect for each other is achieved. There is nothing clever in cheating a witch, for by the very laws of nature, the magick that you require may rebound in some similarly negative way.

7. *Witch's* Bottle
& Cunning Shoe

There are various reports of witch's bottles being used for negative purposes against a witch, but this usage is incorrect. The correct use of a witch's bottle is to protect a person and deflect negative energy. If you are in any way concerned about negative energy being aimed at you but are unsure of what to do, a witch's bottle or cunning shoe may be just the thing to put your mind at rest and resolve the problem. In brief, your sympathetic essence is combined with protective elements and is held inside a glass bottle or shoe. If any negativity is aimed at you, it will instead go to the bottle or shoe that draws this negativity to it through a combination of sympathetic magick and the attraction of your bottled essence. Once drawn to the bottle or shoe, the negativity is defused by the protective elements within. Essentially, it is like having a magnet that pulls all negativity to itself and away from you.

Witch's Bottle

To make a witch's bottle, find a nice glass bottle and a cork that fits tightly into the top. At the time of a New Moon, as the clock chimes the strokes of midnight, rinse the bottle and cork with pure spring water. Place the following elements inside the bottle:

For your essence:
i. a piece of cotton wetted with your saliva
ii. a few of your nail clippings
iii. a hair from your head

In times gone by, urine was used as an essence, but this is not necessary as long as you have at least one of the above three ingredients. The urine spell was also used in witch's bottles for slightly different purposes.

Then put in:

For your protection:
i. A few rusty old iron nails or pins
(which symbolically prick and deflate negativity)
ii. A drop of clove oil (to negate gossip)
iii. A piece of fresh garlic (to exorcise)
iv. A piece of chili pepper (hex breaker)

Taking the bottle in your left hand, raise it up to the new moon and whisper;

"All hex and anger aimed at me,
into this bottle we shall see,
swirling and whirling and trapped in one,
negativity contained will thus be gone."

Now seal the bottle with the cork and place it somewhere in your home where you can forget it in time and leave it to successfully protect you evermore. Witch's bottles of the past are often found bricked up in fireplaces or underneath front door steps. They can be put anywhere within your home where they will not be disturbed.

Cunning *Shoe*

As for cunning shoes, these are predominantly masculine spells, traditionally done for men. Although the overall idea is the same, there are some specific differences. For instance, the shoe used must belong to the man who needs protection. It is stuffed with a variety of ingredients and usually buried at esoteric sites, such as at a crossroads, in sacred water areas, or at the foot of sacred mounds or stones. The reason for this is that the protection is coming from a feminine source (i.e., the areas of the sacred sites). Once the cunning shoe has been placed under this feminine power, the man concerned will be protected by the Goddess wherever he goes and whatever he does.

For his essence:

i. a piece of cotton wetted with his saliva

ii. a few of his nail clippings

iii. a hair from his head, beard, or moustache

For his protection:

i. Dried nettles, rose petals, and a bay leaf (Goddess protection)

ii. Dried dandelion flower and root (specific to Gana, the huntress)

iii. Garlic clove (to exorcise)

iv. Chili Pepper (hex breaker)

v. A flint arrowhead or "Elf Shot" (protection of the Fairy World)

Stuff these ingredients tightly into the shoe and bury it in the desired sacred area. Sit near your offering and, thinking deeply about the words you are reciting, say aloud:

"Goddess, I give you my essence to hold,
In safety and with love's power untold.
Protect your son and draw ever near,
'Ere I stray upon the path of fear.
I heed your advice, protection, and love,
And light fall upon me from thine light above.
It is done. Most blessed be. Amen."

8. Binding

TIE, FASTEN, ATTACH, OR HOLD THINGS TOGETHER

Thread or string and similar lengths such as ribbon or silk represent a line of continuity or a psychic link, which can be magickally fastened between the two worlds of reality and supernatural existence. The knots made within the thread represent various tightly sealed moments in time, the untying of which denotes their release. Knots are tied or untied for specific spellworking practice. Threads chosen in specific colors representing the planets, life forces, and psychic meaning can bind images in restraining spells depending on the substance of the color and magick used.

For example, a knot may be tied in a length of thread of a certain color as a focus for the energy of the Will to complete a corresponding healing spell. Nine knots tied in a red thread and hung around the neck is a basic spell for repelling colds. Knotted ribbons of white or particular colors may be tied around the hands of handfasting couples to symbolically bind their love. Six knots tied in a length of red thread and then woven around a cedar twig and carried within the pocket is a powerful amulet, magickally bound for protection purposes.

9. Banishing & *Smudging*

TO DISMISS OR EXILE A THING FROM ONE'S PRESENCE OR MIND

Banishing is used as a method to repel negativity in extreme cases. It is a form of binding that ensures no return of the negative force, or the placing of that force into a contained field from where it cannot cause an effect. It is similar to exorcism, which is the expulsion of an evil spirit by a command, ritual, or prayer from a person or place. The Romans performed *evocatio*, which was with the exorcism of an entire community rather than an individual. Through their evocatio they would call out the gods of that place, so that they could conquer the evil spirit. During the Second World War a group of renowned mystics threw "go away" powder into the seas for the purpose of repelling Hitler's advances. This can be interpreted as a form of banishing spellwork. Long before medieval times, it was believed that negativity flourished with the aid of water and air. The negativity was forced out by consecrating the water with airborne prayer. The use of holy water against the negative object or person, doubly dispelled it.

Baptism is a way of using holy water in this manner. The terrible maltreatment of witches by using the dunking stool is is also based on this ritual It was believed that if a woman drowned, she was innocent of being a witch and any negativity was returned to the water. If she survived, it was due to the fact that proven witches were able to magickally hold air within themselves. The terrible irony was that the

operators of the dunking stool were actually using magickal theory themselves, which was the very thing they were against. However, due to their ignorance they used the components of a spell to cause harm to others.

Even the ancient Egyptians used a combination of magickal herbs, water, and fire to produce airborne steam in banishing rituals. The idea that air and water are carriers or containers of negativity that can be cancelled out by their own source and can be magickally altered is obviously an old one.

Smudging is a gentler way to disperse negative energy and one that is used any place from one's home to a place used for sacred rituals or spellwork. Smudging requires a mixed bunch of herbs with relevant properties; for example, bay leaf, cedar, rosemary, thyme (purification); angelica, basil, clover, heather (protection); and fern, garlic, mint, or nettle (exorcism). The herbs can be dried naturally when you tie them together with a white ribbon (protection, peace, purification, spirituality) and hang them upside down in a cool, dark place for nine days. During the waxing period of the moon the herbs' powers will increase as they dry.

When the herbs are ready to use, light the tips to produce a thick smoke. Be careful of any flames and always have a bucket of water, a sink, or a stream nearby to dispose of the bouquet if necessary. Wave the smoking bouquet around the area to be smudged, mentally preparing the space for purification and willing any negative energies to disperse. Saying a heartfelt prayer or making a spell while doing this is most effective. When you feel that the area is cleansed to your satisfaction, dispose of the bouquet in water. If the water does not carry the herbs away, throw them backwards over your left shoulder while standing outside.

The processes of banishing and smudging used in spellwork bring together the unconscious and conscious mind to produce a magickal and positive force or Will that repels negativity.

10. Guardian *Spirit*

A HELPER OR MESSENGER FROM THE OTHERWORLD

WHO PROTECTS A PERSON OR PLACE

In the Bible there is mention of angels—such as the Cherubim who were originally the guardians of Eden—who watch over people and places. A guardian spirit is the same thing, but explained without the constraints or boundaries of that particular religious belief. Guardian spirits can be male, female, or asexual. They can be ancestors, animals, fairies such as Dryads or Nymphs, or other creatures. They are essentially a force of goodness, born in spiritual fire, imbued with golden light, and existing in an alternative reality for our safety and spiritual nourishment. Guardian spirits are acquired at a person's birth, although their presence may not initially be felt. The guardian spirit watches over that person and helps when needed. Sometimes they are seen in a vision or dream and at other times their presence is simply felt. A connection to the Otherworld is made and communication can be affected through these guardian spirits.

The Romans recognized three types of guardian spirits. The Genius is essentially a spirit protector of all males. The Juno is a spirit protector of all females. The Genius Loci is a spirit protector of places. These Shining Ones brought divine aid to the people or places they protected.

Although we all have access to a guardian spirit, we don't always invoke it. To connect with your spiritual helper, you must first acknowledge its presence and then, with the power of belief, invoke it into being. Without your involvement, a guardian can become powerless to help you. However, by connecting with this spirit, you become ethereally joined and therefore stronger.

Gaia

Finally, a brief word about the protection of Gaia, our Earth. Although we may be
divided into countries with specific rites and rituals, this Earth is our home, regardless
of artificial boundaries. We should all be free to walk where we want, exchange ideas,
and benefit from our experiences. Sadly, this is not always possible. I have searched for
a protective spell that would correspond to protecting our space, wherever that might be.
If we all concentrate on protecting our individual spaces, the energies might join up with
the universal reflection of love to protect the whole of Gaia. I believe that the best
way to concentrate our energies on protection of our space is to invoke the aid
of three ancient and powerful runic gods. They are Ingwaz, Freya, and Thor.

Ingwaz is the ancient god of Ingland (England), who became known in later times as the
Norse god, Frey. He has healing and protection powers and is invoked in times of national
disaster or danger. He is also connected with solar energy and was known in Saxon times
as the Lord God of Witchcraft. His magickal sigil is the rune ING, named after him.

Freya is the consort of Ing-Frey and is connected with love and magick. She was known
in Saxon times as the Lady Goddess of Witchcraft. Her magickal sigil is the rune CEN.

Thor is a powerful, protective god who is strong, invincible, and loyal to his friends.
Anyone who hurts his friends hurts him, and to his friends he is a masterful warrior
of protection and justice. Thor is the red son of Odin, the shamanic father and ruler of
the Norse gods. He is charged with protecting the Otherworld from its enemies.
His magickal sigil is the rune THORN, which stands for "protector of Asgard,"
the home of the gods. His tree is the blackthorn with all its psychic abilities of banishing,
hex breaking, protection, and power. Thor is an invincible friend and once you connect
to his psychic strength you will have his friendship forever.

PART THREE
Protection

Spells

HESE TEN SPELLS *are of great power and when followed sincerely and with the determination of the Will should bless your life forevermore. They have been taken from different places in the world and from ancient knowledge and practice. I have practiced these spells and found them to be ten of the most useful regarding protection and positivity issues.*

Although seemingly one of the simpler spells, the Su-Su spell, for example, always works extremely well for me and, in fact, was written about by a well-known magazine reporter, who saw it in operation during a visit. The important thing to remember is that it is your determination and belief that will carry these spells forward and make them work. Sometimes it can take some practice and sometimes it will take longer than you imagined, but if your Will is determined and aligned spiritually to the success of a spell, the

Goddess will always respond. To my mind, it is vital when practicing spellwork that you allow yourself to succeed. It is very easy to dismiss a practice if it does not immediately seem to work or reap rewards. However, with perseverance comes understanding and ultimately a deeper knowledge of what you are attempting to achieve.

If you do not allow yourself to succeed, it is very easy to turn that failure into a negative issue. Then, whenever you attempt a spell, the negativity can linger in the ether and affect your spell. Believe in yourself and the power of your Will, for all things are possible if you allow them to be so. Remember that the more you practice a spell, the stronger the essence of that spell becomes. In time the spell can turn into a tangible thing. For example, the silver pentacle that you conjure for protection can become a beautiful image that is as apparent in your home as the paintings on your wall or the carpet on your floor. Perhaps it may be apparent only to you in that special way; however, if you can see it, you are protected by it, and reminding yourself daily or weekly of its presence can only be a good and beneficial experience.

1. TO Protect
Your Home

This is a symbolic ritualistic spell you can do any time you feel the need to protect your home. The more you practice this, the stronger you will feel the protective force. In order for this spell to work well, it is imperative that you concentrate your Will and mind's eye on the success of your spellwork. If you can know in your heart that the spell will work, even before you have started it, you have already succeeded!

You Will Need

1 black candle

1 small dish of salt

1 cinnamon incense stick (if you can't find this, a cactus plant will do instead)

THE METHOD:

• Light the black candle and the incense stick on a table in front of you or place the cactus plant near the candle.

• Sitting comfortably, take deep relaxed breaths, feeling your stomach rising and falling as you do so.

• When you feel you are ready, in your mind's eye draw the image of a five-pointed star (pentagram) with a circle around it (pentacle).

• In your mind see this glowing silver sigil enlarge until it is standing upright in the center of your house.

• Now with all your Will, concentrate on spinning the pentacle (widdershins), slowly at first and then letting it go to continue spinning, radiating its silver light of good fortune and protection throughout your house as it does so.

• Now, stand up and face the front of your house, raise your left arm, and draw the pentacle image in the air in front of you, saying, "I set the Eternal Seal of Protection around me and mine and no one shall enter without my say. It is so. Amen".

• Then turn to the two sides and back of your house and repeat this ritual. Return to the table and blow out the candle saying, "All negative essence be drawn to this candle, dissolve to the black and disperse, never to return, as I make it so. Amen".

• Then take the cup of salt and walk around the main room of your house sprinkling a little in all four corners saying, "Blessed be, protect this house," as you do so.

• Finally, take the burned-down incense and the candle outside and either bury them in earth or throw them in some natural water, knowing that they will take all negativity with them.

• If you have used a cactus plant instead of incense, leave it in your house to draw any negativity to it. Repeat this spell as often as you like to keep the protective magick in force.

2. TO Protect *Yourself* From *Negative Energy*

This spell is worked using the power of the rowan or mountain ash tree, which has strong protective qualities. The tree is commonly found in churchyards and around ancient stone circles due to its sacred nature of protection. It is an amulet for your use.

You Will Need

2 small twigs of the rowan tree

a piece of red silk

a bulb of garlic

THE METHOD

• Find a rowan tree, meditate for a little while to connect with the tree's energy, then ask permission to take two twigs from it.

• When you feel ready, take the twigs and thank the rowan Dryad, leaving a gift of the garlic bulb buried at the base of the tree.

• Now tie the two twigs together into a cross shape with the red silk.

• Take the cross and holding it to the third eye area of your head say, "By the power of the luis bough, spirit calling, I ask that you aid and protect me in all things. Amen."

• You can wear the cross around your neck or in your pocket, or hang it over your home as a powerful protective amulet.

3. TO Protect *Others* from *Negative Energy*

T*his spell is performed using druidess magick and the energy of runic tree work. It is performed outdoors, by a river.*

You Will Need

a sapling wand of holly for each person you wish to protect

a dark gray pen to inscribe sigils upon the wand(s)

a length of red ribbon

a place where a river runs fast

THE METHOD

- Strip a piece of holly sapling to make a bare wand for each person.
- Write upon it with the dark gray pen the name of the person you wish to protect, the EOLH rune sigil which is like the letter "Y" but with the central pole continuing upwards (see illustration), and the name of the god Heimdall, who is the divine ruler of this rune.

- Take the sapling, bend it into a circle, and fasten it securely with the red ribbon.

- Standing on the bank of the river, hold the circlet up to the skies and say, "I call upon the protective aid of Heimdall for my friend's sake, (name of person), and ask that you guard him/her from all unwanted and uncalled for negativity, in this life and the next. My thanks and blessings to thee, O Ruler of the Eolh." Now take the circlet, kiss it three times, and throw it into the fast flowing river.

4. TO Protect
Your Career

In these changing times, the absolute security of one's career can no longer be assured, so it is good sometimes to do this spell to give your working life a boost. This spell is best performed on a Wednesday and incorporates some aspects of Feng Shui (pronounced fung shwee), wind and water magick that is universally recognized.

You Will Need

a large green round-leaved plant

2 small tridents (3-pronged forks)

a magick wand

THE METHOD

For an ideal situation, arrange your office space as follows:

• Your desk should be placed near a wall and you should sit with your back to the wall, facing any doors or windows.

• Place a small trident underneath the two outer corners of your desk and a large, green, round-leaved plant on top of your desk.

• Take a magick wand or use your right hand to ritually point.

• Pointing at any doors or windows in the room, make the pentagram shape with the wand, starting bottom left, up to midpoint, down to bottom right, across to top left, straight across to top right, across and down to bottom left.

• Bring the point of your wand or your index finger inwards to touch your third eye.

• Concentrating on the positive success of your career, chant, "Aaah, Eyyh, Yo," nine times.

• Now clap your hands three times and say, "So be it. Amen."

5. TO Safeguard
a Journey

This spell can be used when setting out on any length of journey, by any means of transport.

You Will Need

a map of your journey (either a published
one or one drawn by yourself)

a blue pen

a cup of fresh spring water

THE METHOD

• Before starting on your journey, take the map of where you are going and in blue ink print these three power words over your destination:

i. Yahsveh

ii. Metatron

iii. Agla

• These three words combine the powers of the Goddess, the guiding angel, and protection.

• Now sprinkle fresh spring water over the map saying, "Agla On Tetragrammaton. Amen."

• Then fold the map in half twice and bury it close to your home. This is the protective force that will work on your behalf as you undertake your journey. It cannot be disturbed because it is held within the earth at the place to which you will safely return.

6. TO Safeguard
Your Health

There are many ways to safeguard your health. Many of us do these things daily without even thinking about it, such as taking vitamins, dressing warmly in cold weather, looking before crossing the road, and so forth. However, sometimes you may feel the need for an extra magickal boost to your health and that is when this spell will come in handy.

You Will Need
a cup of whiskey (known as life water)
a cup of fresh spring water
a twig of ivy
5 kidney beans
a large pot of earth

THE METHOD

• In the pot of earth trace with the ivy twig a stick figure to represent yourself.

• Place a kidney bean on the head, one each on the arms, and one each on the legs, then plant the ivy twig at the top of the stick figure's head.

• Every day for one week at exactly noon, during the time of a waxing moon, sprinkle a little of the whisky (life water) over the figure saying, "Cados, Hagios, Jetros, heal me. Amen," then sprinkle a little of the spring water saying, "Holy, Holy One, Healer, hear me. Amen."

• When the seven days are up, take the pot of earth and hide it outside somewhere where it will not be disturbed, such as a wood or forest.

• Cover it in any bracken or leaves that may be lying about and hide it well.

• You have magickally given yourself a boost of healing, regenerative energy that should continue for some time.

7. TO Safeguard
Your Finances

T*he idea behind this spell is to use the power of the ancient god of plenty, Frey, whose first runic sigil* FEOH *represents wealth (see illustration). This is a form of sympathetic magick, which usually works well. It is always performed outdoors and best done around the latter part of September.*

You Will Need

a silver coin

a piece of ash wood

a piece of green silk

a red ribbon

red ink

a match

THE METHOD

• Perform this magick outdoors, on top of a hill if you can.

• Take the piece of ash wood and inscribe the rune FEOH on it in red ink.

• Now place the silver coin on the wood and wrap them both in the piece of green silk, tying them securely with the red ribbon.

• Make a little hole in the ground and place the parcel in it.

• Now light the match and as it burns, say, "Sacred Frey, I call upon thee with humble respect to witness this act and safeguard my accounts. I ask thee with love for thy magickal blessings upon my wealth and vouchsafe to share all that I have when called upon for the happiness of others. Amen."

• Wait for the match to burn out, place it on top of the parcel, and cover the hole with earth, patting it down hard and removing all traces of any spell work.

8. TO Safeguard
Your Family

The family unit is a very important and loving domain wherein ideally you all care for and help one another. Life can sometimes hit us with hard knocks and there is no absolute certainty of avoiding this, as this is the way of the world. However, on the night of a Full Moon, a nice spell to work for the safeguarding of your family is the following:

You Will Need

a clipping of hair from each family member who is taking part

a red ribbon

some brown paper and sealing wax

a red apple

a silver pin

a cup of spring water

THE METHOD

• Take the hair and tie it together with the red ribbon.

• Slice the top off the apple and hollow out the core space.

• Place the tied hair within it and replace the sliced top.

• Now wrap the apple in the brown paper and seal the joins with the sealing wax.

• Taking the pin, inscribe in the sealing wax a circular spiral, widdershins.

• Let the wax harden.

• Go outside on the night of a Full Moon, hold the parcel up to the moon and say, "Mistress of the Gods, Queen of Heaven, Lady of the World, Great and Dear Mother. I ask thee to safeguard my family in all that they are and in all that they do. Blessed be. Amen."

• By the light of the moon bury the parcel in the ground and sprinkle some spring water over the top, saying, "I ask our Mother's protection forever as we stay within her embrace. Amen."

9. TO Attract
Good Fortune

Good fortune is a powerful state of mind. The people who seem to always be lucky are usually the ones who believe that they will be lucky! People who say they never have any luck will not have much luck because they are stating a negativity that will become fact. The first thing you have to do to attract good fortune is to change your way of thinking and allow yourself to be the receiver of good things! This is a spell to perform when you specifically need to attract good fortune.

You Will Need

a chicken's wishbone

half a lemon

a handful of wild oats

THE METHOD

• Place the wild oats in a bowl and squeeze the lemon into it nine times.

• Stir widdershins nine times with the wishbone saying, "Oats sustain me, lemon cleanses, Good Fortune aid me and attract my senses."

• When done, smear the mixture on your feet, wait for ten minutes, then rinse your feet well and pat dry.

• This glamor will stay about you for approximately half a day, so use its benefits well.

10. TO Banish *a Negative Presence* (Dispersal)

The spell of *Su-Su* pronounced 'Shu shu' is commonly used to banish a negative presence. Shu was the first-born son of the Egyptian god Ra and the goddess Hathor, and the twin brother of the goddess Tefnut. Shu exemplifies the power of light by his act of holding up the sky (Nut) from the earth (Seb) and placing it upon the sacred steps of the city of the eight great cosmic gods. Shu also is known for carrying away hunger from the dead. Shu is often portrayed as a male figure wearing a feather on his head and carrying a scepter. He is usually accompanied by the four pillars of heaven, which represent the four cardinal points. The amuletic image of Shu is usually portrayed as a set of five steps, referring to his light-giving power. By calling on the power of Shu, you are calling on the light and asking for his aid in banishing any negative presence that may be nearby. You can do this spell at any time and in any place, and although it may appear simple in practice, I have found that it is always effective.

• When you are in a situation in which you feel uncomfortable due to a negative presence, simply make the sign of the deer horns in both hands, i.e., index finger and little finger projected, middle and ring fingers and thumbs bent into palm of hand, and keep them hidden from view in your pockets.

• Concentrate hard on the area where you feel or see the negative presence and say very loudly and firmly in your mind, "Shu, Shu, Shu."

That is all. The power comes from knowing that once you have done this, the spellwork will take effect and you will be free from any negative presence. If by any chance the feeling or person is so persistent that it doesn't go away within five minutes, do the ritual again. You may need to concentrate harder on the force of the words. This spell can also be used for minor things, such as traffic jams or lines that are holding you up. However, as with all spellwork, you should not use the ritual so often that it becomes commonplace, otherwise the intensity of the magick may be lessened.

Epilogue

Fly forward now to the present day as we work. War is in retreat, Disease and Despair have turned against their friend, and Cabal is being rediscovered, unearthed from its early tomb and carefully dusted down by the children of the children who went before. Our Ancestors are being worshipped again. Cautiously she reappears, bringing forth her secrets and making sense to those that have found her. Venus, Flamen, and Laetitia watch from their hidden place, too early to rejoice, yet they know that the female power is making her return to the World. And when she prevails, Most Blessed Be, they know, too, of the splendors that will come. The golden light prepares to circulate again and in doing so begins its return to the Creative. Through this action we can all see the way of ascent and joining to the One, the great primordial spirit in the first city of Cabal, reborn from the ashes. May the light of the Golden Flower circulate for you too, always and evermore.